PLASMA

PITT POETRY SERIES
Ed Ochester, Editor

BRADLEY PAUL

UNIVERSITY OF PITTSBURGH PRESS

Published by the University of Pittsburgh Press, Pittsburgh, Pa., 15260
Manufactured in the United States of America
Printed on acid-free paper
10 9 8 7 6 5 4 3 2 1

ISBN 13: 978-0-8229-6559-6

COVER ART: Melissa W. Miller, *Anima*, 1996. Chine-collé line etching with spit bite and sugar lift aquatint, 19 1/2 x 25 in. Courtesy of the artist.
COVER DESIGN: Joel W. Coggins

FOR VIOLET AND STELLAN

CONTENTS

I. Moments of Intrigue in Language Acquisition

II. Eleven Questions on the Deaths of Animals

III. Obituaries and Other Pastimes

PLASMA

MOMENTS OF INTRIGUE IN LANGUAGE ACQUISITION

I bring out the old manual mower.
My son, four months,
sits on the porch
on his mother's lap.
The mower clanks and whooshes.
The blades are dull.
I push three feet forward,
two feet back,
three forward.
My son furrows
his infant brow.
He shouts.
A baby bark.
I smile at him.
He shouts again.
I say, Hello!
Then he wails.
He is afraid of the mower.
It is the first time
he has shown fear.

He will dream of this one day.
I have dreamt it.
Something horrifying,
your father behind a machine
that does not slash but rips
with dull and incessant blades.
You shout to stop it

but your father just smiles.
Or your son crawling
into the surge of the nighttime sea,
or your dog ignoring
your command to come in
and then your plea,
staring into the darkness of the yard
then walking into it
and in the morning there is nothing
but grass.
Your shouts do nothing.
You do not have the word Stop
or any other word
to stop anything.
This, son, will happen often.

The lawns will not be green for long
but no one believes it.
When you have water you think
I will always have water.
It's right here
and there's more in the pipes
and the pipes have always run.
Run is what pipes do.
Once, asleep, I hoped:
I am sleeping now,
I know I am,
and if I am sleeping now
maybe I always will.
This in the back
of my grandfather's Oldsmobile
as I was being driven to be dropped off
someplace awful.
Maybe the ride will just go on.
An eternal Now,
the stars like pins holding up
the drooping black upholstery of night.
But it was only ten minutes
and then I had to get out.
It was as bad
as I expected.
The Olds is gone, and the old folks too.
I got some money out of that
and for a while I thought

now I've finally got money.
Got. Got. Got.
That's what water is,
like money:
you finally have it and think
how could I have ever not?
Look at me affording things.
Look at me water the lawn.
Then it's all
gone again.
Tapped out, ha.
Water is like money.
I say *money* because
I was recently broke
and still fear it.
But what I mean is,
like everything.

The boy of me falls on his butt
and cries *oh, butt!*
Or throws the little wooden train
and cries *oh no!*
As if: *how did that happen?*
The boy of me learns how to say
I'm mad!
and so says it all the time
even when he's not.
The boy of me learns.
He touches an older boy, *hello*,
and the older boy hits him.
The boy of me doesn't know
if he remembers this
or imagines it,
but knows it happened,
remembers it
when a smaller child touches him,
hello.
He should hit him now, he thinks.
Then does.
An adult somewhere says
use your words.
But the boy of me has
only so many words.
He lives in *house.*
The burger place
is *fries house.*

The outdoor toilet at the park
is *potty house.*
He is himself a house of words
and the words themselves are each a house
of something he has seen or felt.
House of *angry,*
house of *moon.*
But what does *of* mean?
He cannot see *of.*
He has learned a word
he cannot throw,
a word on which
he cannot fall.
How did that happen?
He is mad because
there are more words every day.
Some, he has learned,
will get him hurt
and some will get his
little wooden train picked up.
Which is *of?*
He cannot know until
of has a picture.
So he says
he is of the ocean.
Of as in *came from*
or *belongs to*
or *is made of.*

Because he has seen the ocean.
He tastes the salt on his lips.
I can taste the salt on his lips.
So few words for all these words but
the boy of me makes do.

They are not flowers of the lips;
they are whispers.

It is not fear;
it is a stone.

Is it your flesh?
Or merely a chair?

Have you asked
or have you demanded?

You haven't turned blue
but merely drunk;

you haven't turned wild
but iron.

And here you sit waiting
for the great reckoning,

the final accounting
for every mistake ever,

whispering to people
at tables nearby

are you a criminal
or merely with me?

are you all colors
or only red?

But all that comes
is a bill for what you drank.

You've long since drained the cup
but at the bottom

remains a stone,
and in the stone

a red streak of iron,
your fear.

A monk scraping off
the black letters of Galen
and adding the red of Christ.
Bodies skinned
but for a purpose.
The vellum remembers
the calf it was.

The actors want their lines
but the writer is distracted by a new word:
gallicantu.
Meaning cock's crow.
Cantus of the gallus.
A mass at gallicantu,
stealing milk at gallicantu,
filming at gallicantu
in gallicantu's perfect blue
which puts everything in relief
like the raised black hash mark
at the end of a plastic ruler,
the 300th millimeter, across from
the 96th eighth of an inch.
Ending, finitude, incongruous measures:
is there some way to add this
to the script?
How about a guy
who tries to be a cult leader
but isn't charismatic enough.
How about a cat lady
who has no cats.
How about a gaffer who's been here long enough
to remember Betty Grable's legs
insured for a million bucks.
The gaffer says the money's
is the only opinion that counts
and the money, writer, doesn't like you.
Gallicantu. Gallicantu.

Without resorting to Wikipedia I know
that archaeopteryx is a dinosaur bird.
I think it had feathers.
Most dinosaurs did, didn't
I read?
I assume it laid eggs and preyed
on the eggs of others.
But already I'm guessing.
It's shameful.
We should be able to write poems
without the internet.
So let me say also that archaeopteryx
is a word I used as a kid
to sound smart
and as an adult for jokes.
Dry jokes where a big word works,
"look what unexpected reference
I just plucked from the æther,"
emphasis on æther's
arch little steampunk ligature.
Smart jokes that people
with thick plastic glasses make.
Reduced to jokes,
dinosaurs are anymore,
and also plastic glasses.
And little creamer cups.
And an injectable polymer
that stops soldiers from bleeding to death.

And civilians as well if they're bleeding.
You can imagine the reasons why.
No need to be graphic.
But maybe a fight over lust
or football or who
said what about someone
and a steak knife was close
and now it's all sentencing
and regret
that no one believes.
And of course gas.
Dinosaurs make gas.
I burned three velociraptors
just getting to Target.
Wait: that's not funny
or true.
Plastic and petroleum
don't actually come from dinosaurs.
"Fossil" fuel is a misdirect.
They come from microplankton
which, as it decomposed into oxygen,
nitrogen, phosphorous, and sulfur,
left a combustible sludge
of carbon and hydrogen.
Okay, *that* I looked up.
I didn't want to sound stupid.

In hindsight everything was an omen.
You mess with the king and everyone dies
like in all those Shakespeares.

The egg with no yolk.
The mantis in winter.
You open the breadbox
but find only the knife.
Augurs, all of them,
but we were worrying about the flies,
which don't show what will happen
but what already has.

The Landscape Gallery Is the Gallery Everyone Skips

In a valley of pines
nothing else can grow.

And a wood of elms
is a wood of parasites.

Can we see the bark beetles?
Or the acid in the earth?

Or is it enough
that they get the light right.

My Son Says He Is Making an Animal

It has no trunk because
he does not want an animal with a trunk.
Also, no eyes. It should not see.
Also, no mouth. Also, no ears.
Though he just said no mouth
he adds: no teeth, either.
No head, actually,
and no tail.
No feet. And no body.
That's the animal he wants.
I tell this to another adult
and we laugh until we realize
the playground is hot
and we've been so long in the sun
we can't escape it.
Acre of black rubber ground.
The heat warps the air
inside the single jungle gym.
Wait: I know this animal.
I adopted it from a shelter
that had no cages.
I thought it was nothing
until it pissed inside the house.
What summer is this,
with no leaves on the trees?

I'd kill myself
if it weren't so permanent.
Illegitimate poetry. You,
for whom legitimacy is a thing.
My son in the living room says *poyple*
but tomorrow will say *purple* like everyone else.
The lights dip when the air comes on.
Blackness enough to lose something.

In The City of Black Currants a widower drinks all the black currant juice because it calms his grief. By law he must now make more juice from a basket of seven currants.

In the first currant he sees his wife in a kitchen chair thinking something he can't guess. In the second he sees his wife in a bikini in Hawaii. In the third he sees his wife angry. The fourth, his wife happy. The fifth, his wife holding hands with his grandmother. The sixth, he sees himself always watching his wife. His wife his wife his wife.

He can't bear to look into the seventh so the widower writes a letter. Invites a distant friend to lunch. Tells him about the juice, the chair, the bikini, how he saw his wife in a currant though he feared she was in Hell. Asks him, Does this kind of thing happen there?

The friend reads the letter. Yes, it happens here. He himself looked into the seventh currant and saw his own wife saying, a City of Black Currants cannot exist; I am in Hell. All your fears are correct.

How should I reply, the friend thinks. How should I reply.

ELEVEN QUESTIONS ON THE DEATHS OF ANIMALS

The bald kind. The rat teeth kind.
Is it sad to sleep all that much
or is it nothing?

The pretty boy in pomade forever
with a pretty girl agog.
The boy by the ocean
all Ferris wheel and hair.
No.

You are the black felt kind against
more black felt.
The scissors kind, the paper kind.
The kind who transports
all that dirt.
Everyone on the ship is dead,
and that's just fine with you.

That kind. Sarcastic. Sardonic.
Wherever did you find the shoes
to match those smarty pants?
You're a *fine* friend.

From the Greek *sarkasmos*:
to tear flesh,
to bite the lips in rage,
to sneer.
To line your kiss with shark's teeth.
To snip the rose before it blooms
so the thorns grow sharper and long.
And from these you make
a pair of socks for Sally Earnest,
underwear
for Literal Joe.
Tone deaf,
their skin's been threshed,
they're in love.

Get some rocks.
Now stack the rocks.
Now seal the rocks.
Now run some water
over the rocks.
The piscinae fill
with your favorite fish.
Just like all the people.
There are fish
in their fishbowl eyes.

That's the kind of emperor you are.
Public works guy.
Crown of laurel guy.
Succeeded by a madman
so the people love you
that much more.
Look at the coins they minted:
Your face on one side.
A fish on the other.
The fish that draws
a cart of palms.
The fish that bears a bridle.
So substantial and leaden
beside the wall of rosemary.
Look at all this water!

What Kind of Second Are You?

You are the twenty-third second.
Between the twenty-second second,
in which the man fell into the lake,
and the twenty-fourth second,
in which he stood up, sputtering and wet.
A mile away from the twenty-fifth second,
of people concerned,
a light year from the twenty-sixth,
of people laughing.
The second of minnows mid-arc
between fleeing the splash
and seeing what food might have fallen to them.

Even in another minute
away from the lake,
even in a desert,
you are always only this,
a gradual sense of green,
a solid in a liquid,
no memory yet of falling,
no anger that you fell.

He is in the acacia, laughing.
But there are more than six hundred
types of acacia,
some called false acacia,
or umbrella or bullhorn or sugar.
Some used as incense,
some to ward off ghosts.
They sit in the nursery
waiting to be sorted,
breaking already
through their black plastic pots
into the black asphalt lot.
Once we are gone
it won't take long at all.
I have no name
for the bird I saw,
the bird with yellow throat
laughing in the blue tree.

I'm rooting for Belgium
because of their fries.
No, I'm rooting for Slovenia
because of their statues of poets.
No, I'm rooting for Deutschland
because of käsekuchen.
No, I'm rooting for Italy
because Il Corriere loves American TV.
No, I'm rooting for Angola
because it seems about time for them.
No, I'm rooting for Mexico
because of the days of their dead.
No, I'm rooting for Ethiopia—
lions, stand up!
Come out of the forest and free us
from their aquariums and tongues,
lions, o lions, o lions.

What Kind of Psychic Soccer Octopus Are You? 2

But what is this team in orange?
Oh, them, says the octopus.
I like them too.
They are like the orange of the tavern lights
that I see from my tank, he says.
They are like the orange of sixty-watt light
outside my closed eyelid, I say.
Intriguing, says the octopus.
We both of us see
through a skin on our eyes.
Do you mean the water
or the glass of the tank? I ask.
Either one, he says. Or both.
But it doesn't matter.
Look at that *orange*.

What Kind of Decay Are You?

Something about this room is off.
The timbre of its air.
The flavor of its existence.
Foreign, like other people's groceries:
this woman buys only that hippie bread
that has to be kept in the refrigerator;
that man eats pickled pearl onions.
Here's a family that drinks Mr. Pibb.
Their sweat tastes different
and the microbes that eat their sweat
smell different when they die
and fall with the skin flakes
into the rugs and mattresses.
They look so similar but
the death of your skin is different
from the death of my skin.
Your home is a coffin of weird.

What Kind of Suspension Are You?

Refused entrance
to your own grave.
No reason. No reason.
Not so funny now
except to everyone else.
You feel as if you're dressed in curtains,
an unlight man
next to the reflecting pool
beshat by Canada Geese,
while your angel of a dog
begs you eternally
to eat, to walk,
to chase a squirrel into the afterlife
or any other life.

What Kind of Childish Fantasy Are You?

There is a heaven and
there are animals there.
The ones you let live in your house
and also the ones you killed.
Spiders in the sofa.
Every pig you ate bacon from.
The dog you could not save.
Is it a jungle
or is it a farm,
this heaven you wish to see
where all your animals stare.

What Kind of Groundcover Are You?

When my dog Violet died
someone gave us violets.
I thought, She's transformed!
And planted the violets
so she could always play
amid the mess of clover.
Don't step on the dog! I say
to anyone walking through
though actually people
don't go back there anymore.

What Kind of Meteorology Are You?

The local news is dumb but local.
Who cares about a mugging
except I know that corner.
It will rain, so what,
except it rains on me.
The first drop
is a heavy one.
The cotton where it lands
is heavy on my shoulder
but the rest of the cotton is light.
My shirt grows heavy too now,
says the weather girl.
A warehouse near here burned
but only partially.
The shadow of one helicopter moves left
as the light of another moves right.
I know that warehouse,
and here it is on TV burning
as it rains first on one fireman
then on the next.

What Kind of Person Were You?

Waiting in line for Charon.
Wild thyme grows
on the gray and igneous ground.
Purple flowers.
Guy ahead of me says,
What are you in for?
I am dour because I just died
and won't look up from the thyme.
My kidneys have shut.
My khakis fill with blood.
This is Hades, not Hell,
I say. We all come here
no matter what we did.
I know, says the guy.
That's the joke.

OBITUARIES AND OTHER PASTIMES

One death tugged up by another
like Kleenex from a bottomless box.

Mourners blowing their noses
on each of the infinite deaths!

But the obituaries,
there's only one guy who writes these.

He takes notes
as he walks to work:

death as a rotten little sandwich,
death as a tarry roof.

As a tangerine leaf
rubbed into the wooden crate.

As the scatter of dirt
at the crate's bottom.

As the book you signed out as a child
still on the shelf

though the library is gone. Death
as the way you signed your name as child.

It is only the way that persists,
not the signature itself.

And already he is at his office door,
which today is painted blue.

Wide Is the Gate, Narrow the Way

Tour bus on a high narrow road.
Amalfi.
Driver got too casual,
too Italian.
Cell phone, cigarette.
Rolls the bus.
Now everyone will die
earlier than they thought.
Upside down, too.
Except as they fall
one man is already dead.
Died just after boarding.
Looked asleep.
A corpse on tour
over the lemon terraces
now tumbling
in a busful of corpses-soon-to-be.
He feels a bit of seniority and smiles
in that immobile corpse way.
My eternity, he thinks,
will forever be a half hour
longer than theirs.

Samuel Beckett Driving Andre the Giant to School

Like the voice of Abraham Lincoln
or the first Viking guitar
or the beating of a pterodactyl's wing:
one wishes a tape recorder had been there.
Perhaps it was beautiful
or perhaps just history.
Or not even history but
a curio from an interesting age,
popular among the geeks
who plan science museums
and the schoolteachers who love them.
There go two of them now,
sneaking off to share a Sprite
in the echoes and purple light
beyond the stuffed mastodon,
that mammoth frozen
so deeply and perfectly
that when it was found ten feet inside a glacier
they fed its meat to their dogs.

It rained, and I almost saw
my grandmother's wooden walls

swelled in their every cell
by radiator and cigarettes,

and warm. And
some kind of bird

red in my ken
until I turned to see it.

And the tree of what I know
was never there.

We wanted the joke
to be on them again.

We want the joke
to be on them.

I went to sit
but they stole my chair.

Where it had sat on the linoleum
four light spots

and above them
standing me

who wants revenge, magical
weight-bearing plank.

I can't remember if I wrote it or read it but
there was another poem saying
Everyone dies! Everyone dies!
like a whiny gothy cockatiel.
Hey, Poem:
we know.

I once saw a cockatiel
under some honeysuckle.
Escaped? Feral?
I don't know but
hurt, definitely.
Something with the wing.
I thought about saving it
but do people really save birds?
Who would I call?
This was in Texas,
cruel and stupid, insentient
and indifferent to sentience.
Or maybe I'd return it to health myself,
and reap his loyalty
and cell phone chirps –

but by the time I looked again
the mourning doves had found it.
The dun little psychopaths plucked his eyes
and then his crest and then watched
until the cat came.

Poem, stop being a cockatiel
because this is what awaits you.
Nature's a fuck
and no one buys your moping.
We are all Texas to you.
The whole deal, Poem, is that
you'll outlive the writer.
One of those clichés that's true.
So get over yourself.
Get a lapdance. Or go to Rome.
Yes, we're all dying, but you,
you're living the life.
Or could
if you'd just shut up.

They'll take it from a dead cow or,
where market dictates, man.

The worse you are
the more you'll need.

Do not believe those
Korean horror movies;

you will not wake
with the cow's memory of

yellow kernels
in a steel trough,

nor egret craning
upon her neck.

You will not one day driving have
the dead man's memory of the breath of the girl

he spoke to only once
before leaving forever a turreted town

painted everywhere
with skeletons and Christs

but of which he remembers only
the taste of the sea on her breath,

this kernel of breath
in the brain of the man

who was cheaper
than a cow,

who bobs in a vat
with the other donated dead,

this corpse to be grafted onto you,
who have minorly cracked your skull,

afloat and unfixed, thinking
What? What? What?

The silver nitrate takes a while.
The daughter's set on a chair.
Now, while she still has eyes.
The mother stands, alive
but no less still.

spelled SURRENDER DOROTHY
and now it won't come off.

Funny thing, says the praying mantis,
is actually I'm an atheist.

Yet there are so many flies to eat.
Corpse of the flying monkey.

::CAUTION EXOTIC ANIMALS::

Unzooed
into Ohio's nothingness and rain.

This is what they mean by noir,
the stomach
like a bag of lead peaches
(that's how caution feels);
a tiger in a kiddie pool.

I closed the window. The air conditioner
was cold but whirred like brakes.
Was cold but rattled like brakes.
Rattled like brakes and was warm.
Was quiet and the room was hot.

I opened the window. Saw headlights
on the mountain road.
Headlights on the mountain's side.
Saw headlights falling. Then darkness
and the smell of gasoline.

The mountain sits between my house
and the ocean. Some days
it blocks the breeze. Other days
the breeze surmounts the mountain.
Brings coolness and filth from the ocean.

A woman you've never seen before blows in.
She is a container of cold.
Like a house. Like a truck.
Like the ocean.
Perfume of flame and filth.

Unfathomable, but
who uses fathoms anymore?
A man climbs into a ghost
and wonders where the fear is.

I Want to Think but the TV's On

It packs my head
with its slurry of tiny drama.

The fisherman
dragged into the water.

His buddy yells
Swim, Charlie,

take my word for it,
don't look back, Charlie,

swim!
But Charlie looks back.

Like Lot's wife, like Orpheus,
like everyone.

He's not in the water anymore
nor is his buddy a fisherman.

Nor is there a shark
nor is he Charlie.

What show was I on, thinks
the character, what channel?

It was an apartment.
It was full of tiny drama.

Did the shark kill them all?
Did I?

He wonders if it's a comedy.
He swims wonderfully in the plasma.

Giant clams can live five hundred years.
There is right now off Massachusetts
one over whom pitched the Mayflower.
A yellow scuba arm trapped
in the massive lip's hard ruffle.
Inside, a pearl from pilgrim dirt.

I sense someone named Joe. John.
A J name. Or R.
I sense he is angry. Or not.
He was angry. At least once.
Perhaps he is angry again,
or ready to be.
Did you do something
to offend this ghost?
Did you say his name wrong
or not at all?
Did you spend the dime of his you found
when you scraped the painted floor?
He is saying do not worry
and do.
He wants you to eat
and doesn't.
He wants you to feel the weight
of black bread in your stomach
and hunger for black bread,
perpetually and simultaneously,
as he does,
and to guess at names,
as he does,
this ghost who can't remember
of whom he is a ghost.

Squirrel skulls
on which the smaller demons sit.

A spade left standing
against the massive radiator.

The buffalo's horn
unworn.
Actually red
from not being rubbed.
Unused
like so little else.
And now in a plastic case, faced
with the faces of the slaughtered.
A coin so valuable
it can't be spent.

The collector, tired
of obvious ironies.

How cool I would be
if I carried a machete everywhere.
If I owned a cuckoo clock.
If I paid with Eisenhower dollars.

If I put the head of Eisenhower
into the cuckoo clock.
I wake up and realize
this is what the machete is for.

The head of Eisenhower
sings on the hour.
The cuckoo sits
on the window ledge.

It still sings Edelweiss
but at irregular intervals,
irrespective of Eisenhower's head.
The shadows outside grow irregularly,

here lopped off by moonlight,
here by the wall of the school
where the children still wait for the bell,
flipping their headless coins.

I bought this cuckoo clock
and it is very modern.
It isn't a cuckoo but
a naked woman every hour
and she says
Remember me?
Remember me?
We saw a shark together.
It swam beneath the kitchen floor.
It was our house
but not our house.
Familiar
but unfamiliar.
An almost-shark,
mouth of saltwater
but also mouth of lemon.
The crease where her thigh
meets her hip when she sits –
barely do I remember the naked woman
when she is gone again behind the little door
with the little bellows
and the little gears
attached to little chains
that run down to the pine cone weights,
except they're not pine cones
but little naked men
who speculate about the living room before them
and to what their chains are attached

and with every minute
figure out another thing.
But it is hourly almost the hour.
Little men, when you hear
Remember me?
twelve times in a row
you will know that it's noon,
and you will forget
everything you know,
a simple fact you've known for a minute
but for another minute now know better.

Shirts I bought ten years ago.
Some still have my dog's hair on them.
Fake pearl buttons were briefly a thing.
In such a shirt I thought
I should move to Los Angeles.
In Los Angeles now I think
the real Los Angeles
is two zip codes away.
Had we been happy?
Are we now?
Blood of an animal thinks
it is an animal itself.
Does not understand why it's moving.

Mysterious Orphan Appears on Page 30.
Possessed or Just Insane?

Bakelite eyes.
Balafon bones.
Teeth whittled
into miniature skulls
that themselves
have whittled teeth.
Hungry but
can bite so little.

Fuck you.
Fuck me?
Fuck you.
Okay. Anything
else?
Fuck everyone.
The stoplight clicks.
A mockingbird at 2 AM.
Someone's going to kill this bird
if only they could see him.
Fuck everyone.
Okay, sir.
I'll tell them.

Opening Lines for a Potentially Wonderful Novel

I'd never killed an accountant before.

He knew from the first word which character he would kill.

So many people died that month that it had started to get boring.

My big idea was to pay to get a star named after her and as big ideas go that one's pretty small.

Walter Jensen had gotten pretty good at guns.

Rudeness had always come naturally to him.

Being rude was easy for Walter Jensen.

Walter Jensen woke up with emphysema.

The last vampire in town was having a pretty good time of it.

He had teeth like a row of urinals.

He had teeth like a shelf of raisin bread.

He had teeth like a squabble of pigeons.

He had just gotten dentures.

Walter Jensen's body was blocking the sprinkler.

"We got company," said the bombardier. But Walter Jensen's earpiece was dead.

The general opinion was that the mayor was lousy, but there'd be plenty of tuna anyway.

The general opinion was that the mayor was lousy, but a good mayor would be worse.

She was the kind of dame that lugs like Walter Jensen would call *built for regret.*

The raccoons all had human eyes.

Of people whose father died this year I know five, including myself.

I could tell right away the kid was sharp as a baloney sandwich.

It was noon but morning light still hung in the ossuary.

Walter Jensen had killed all the flies and now the spiders were starving.

They cast Walter Jensen as a Roman, as they did every Easter.

If you don't want pregnant fish then you'd best have no fish at all, Walter Jensen thought as the July sun bleached the tops of his tomatoes.

There are many types of people in the world but the two that interest me are the living mostly and the dead on occasion.

If it hadn't been for the turtles they would have razed the house already but the turtles were there and you couldn't damn well pretend they weren't.

He could tell his legs had gotten weaker.

There's a common belief among undertakers that the dead don't know they've died but at the moment of death just seamlessly continue in the afterlife what they'd been doing.

Walter Jensen stood next to the cherrywood box and thought, Those are my father's ashes in there and that's pretty much all there is to it.

That summer the museum was robbed; most of what they got were reproductions.

Young Walter Jensen put his gun back in his waistband and thought he'd better get out of there before the really bad guys got there and showed him what he'd done wrong.

There is a flower that grows in Hell called the Widower's Rose.

There is a rose that grows in Hell called Brilliant Sulfur.

There is an orchid that grows in Hell that only Satan may pluck.

There is an orchid that grows in Hell that Satan waters.

All this talk of hell, thought Walter Jensen, and yet none of the ghosts say anything.

There were devils in the pantry, but they were indistinguishable from dust or angels or dark.

Bedtime Story

The coyote says Fuck this sunlight,
I can't tell the mice from the sand.

The possum says Fuck this broken phone line.

The goat says Fuck this picnic table,
I'll stand on something else.

The roach says Fuck this stove.

The rose finch says Fuck the golden finch
who has eaten all my cashews.

The bear says Fuck this sleep.

The giraffe says Fuck this view,
he can see the lion cursing the chase,

cursing the grass too short to hide him,
cursing the pigs safe in their hutch,

cursing the piglets
too young to curse.

So much pollen
atop so much dust.
Cleaning just makes it worse.

We walked on a field
then built on a field.
Homes and baths
built of field stone.
Little terraces
of terrazzo made.
Every night the thud
of a falling lemon.
It lies on the terrace,
split and drying.

Stratum of gold
upon stratum of gray.
In a thousand years
they dig up our sneeze.

Microns wide like the little graves
of the fleas fleas have.
Between them, the smallest view of sea.

Not in disparate molecules waiting to fission or fuse, nor in fat waiting to congeal (fat doesn't anticipate, is aware only of its present fatness, this is the genius of indulgence), nor in any way at all except for its readiness to appear.

This is what I hate about milk: its propensity for metaphor.

To my God, who expected more: I am sorry I am slow.

Disclosures for the Home I'm Selling

Coyotes get on the roof.
That's where they take their rabbits.
You will lie there listening.
The blood stays in the shingles.

From the front porch
you will hear five languages spoken.
Of these you will understand English.
The rest we have been in wars with.

My son speaks more every day
but I get deafer.
We will align for just one day
where I hear all of what he says

but not more. Our voices
like our blood briefly
will with one another be exact,
each of my blood cells

banging its iron at him,
each of his banging back.
We will not know what it means
but we will understand.

Some of these poems first appeared in the following journals:

American Poetry Review, B O D Y, Drunken Boat, InDigest, North American Review, 42opus, and *5 AM.*